Poppyland in Pictures

Elizabeth Jones

Introduction

Before illustrating the attractions of "Poppyland" it is perhaps necessary to set the scene, to establish where it was and to show what the area was like prior to the 1880's. Cromer is described in a guide book of the 1850 s as a quiet and select "watering-place," with the advantages of a "salubrious and invigorating air, a fine and open sea" and extremely "pleasing scenery." White's Directory of the same period commented that since 1785, the town had improved so considerably that, "it now ranks as one of the most fashionable sea-bathing places in the kingdom."[1] The arrival of the railway in 1877 attracted more visitors, and yet a guide book of 1880 noted that Cromer lacked the necessary spirit of speculation in building to make it a successful holiday resort. In the same era, Sheringham was said to be an "unspoilt and old-fashioned area, in which "the modern villa was still conspicuous by its absence."[2] Overstrand and Sidestrand too were quiet and quaint, unaware of the "invasion" that was to begin in 1883.

When Clement Scott, a writer with the "Daily Telegraph," arrived in Cromer on an assignment on August Ist of that year, he thought the town to be, "perhaps the prettiest watering-place of the East Coast."[3] However, Scott found the routine rather dull and the crowds tiresome, and he soon discovered a place more to his taste during a ramble along the cliff-top. Sidestrand, with its crumbling cliffs and fields dotted with poppies, appeared to the journalist seeking solace from the bustle of London to be a paradise, the "haven" he had been yearning for. A series of articles were prepared under the title, "Poppyland - by a Holiday-maker, written at a farmhouse by the sea." These articles proved to be so popular that Scott later published them in a volume entitled "Poppyland Papers descriptive of scenery on the East Coast," in 1886.

Clement Scott, born in London in 1841, was a highly influential writer by the 1880's, especially in the field of dramatic criticism, where he was hailed as "the pioneer of picturesque style."[4] Scott's poem, "The Garden of Sleep," caught the imagination of the public, and once the words had been set to music by Isidore de Lara it became one of the most popular songs of the day. Following a flood of letters from people who loved the song, but were mystified by the lyrics, the author wrote further on the subject in 1890, combating the "charge of idiocy on the one hand and drug-imbibing on the other."[5] He simply explained that the poem referred to a forgotten graveyard on the Sidestrand cliffs, with an old church tower, and that poppies were a symbol of death. The song and the book led to the area becoming so popular that ten years later Scott regretted telling the World about his "haven of rest and peace."[6] In the "Norfolk Post" of 1932 it was claimed that "Clement Scott's articles, coupled with the opening of the railway to North Norfolk, started the movement which finally made Cromer a fashionable seaside resort."

The farmhouse by the sea to which Scott referred in his writing was the Mill House at Overstrand, later renamed "Poppyland House," where he stayed with the miller and his daughter, Louie Jermy. Time and again the writer returned to the Mill House, bringing a host of literary personalities such as Swinburne, Theodore Watts-Dunton, and George Sims to stay there. They too must have become caught up in the aura of Poppyland, for Swinburne was inspired to write "A Midsummer Holiday" there, and Sims often wrote of the area under the name "Dagonet" in his "Mustard and Cress" columns in "The Referee." Watts-Dunton wrote his classic "Aylwin" whilst staying at the Mill House. The miller's daughter also became somewhat of a celebrity through her hospitality towards her famous guests, being nicknamed "Louie of the Blackberry Puddings" by George Sims.

Poppyland is an area that is hard to define, for in a wide sense, the whole of the East coast of Norfolk and Suffolk could be referred to in this manner. According to Scott, who after all was responsible for the name, his "haven" would seem to have centered around Sidestrand and Overstrand, but also included Cromer, Sheringham, Mundesley, Yarmouth and Lowestoft. Once the area had become famous, the Poppyland image, in the form of postcards and souvenirs, was used to attract more visitors. Local railway companies took up the idea, and not only made use of the theme in advertisements, but even opened a "Poppy-Line" from Cromer to Mundesley. The late 1880's and early 1890's saw a great influx of visitors into the area, accompanied by a boom in the building of hotels and private residences.

Overstrand became known as the "Village of Millionaires" in the late 19th century, owing to the many famous people who bought property in the area. The example of Lord and Lady Battersea, who purchased a home in the village, was copied by others such as Sir Edgar Speyer, Sir John Hare and Sir George Lewis, all of whom bought or built homes there in that era. The population of Overstrand increased from 253 to over 400 between the 1860's and 1890's, whilst that of Cromer soared from 1,597 in 188l to 3,781 in 1901. Sheringham also shared in the popularity brought by Scott and the accessibility brought by the railways; the population there rose by over 300 from the 1880's to the late 1890's.

Following the success of Scott's articles about the area, in the 1890's the "Lady's Pictorial" sent Mrs. A. Berlyn and the artist W. W. Russell to Overstrand to investigate his claims. The outcome of their stay was a book entitled, "Vera in Poppyland," from which originated the phrase "Scotto-mania." This widespread disease, from which one of the book's characters suffered, began with the urge to sing "The Garden of Sleep" constantly, followed by a desire to buy souvenirs and postcards, and a need to re-visit the Mill House on frequent occasions. It was publicity such as this that prompted the newspaper comment in 1914 that "The name Poppyland is here to stay," but was it?

Even in 1890, Scott had written, "The Cromer that we visit now is not the Cromer I wrote about but a few short years ago as my beloved Poppyland;" he felt his Poppyland to be doomed, wishing he had kept it to himself to prevent it from becoming "not Poppyland, but Bungalow Land."[7] G. C. Harper called the Cromer of the early 20th century "the Motor Cad's Paradise," whilst a letter in the "Cromer and North Walsham Post" complained of "the lamentable state of affairs at your beautiful resort." Despite the fact that the old church tower in Sidestrand fell over the cliffs in 1916, the image was still used on postcards up till the 1930's. Scott died in 1904, Louie Jermy in 1934, and yet the Poppyland legend was still thought worthy of mention in the guide books of the 1950's. Even though the image of Poppyland has faded today, the popularity of the area continues, and thousands of visitors enjoy holidays on the North Norfolk coast.

Notes:

1. "White's Directory," W. White. (1845)
2. "Reminiscences," Lady Battersea. (1922)
3. "Poppyland," Clement Scott. (1886)
4. "The National Biographical Dictionary."
5. "Blossom Land and Fallen Leaves," Clement Scott. (1890)
6. "Poppyland," Clement Scott. (1886)
7. Clement Scott, c.1900

Foreword

Elizabeth Jones graduated with a B.A. in English and History from King Alfred's College, Winchester. A family home in Cromer and time as volunteer helper at Cromer Museum have given her the background knowledge of the Poppyland story, a series of events that changed the face of North Norfolk.

The idea for putting these pictures together for the centenary of the opening of the story in 1883 began with the many requests for a book with the pictures discovered by Jarrold and Sons in the basement of their Cromer shop and displayed in Cromer Church for the summer of 1981. To these have been added pictures from the Cyril Crawford Holden collection, a number of which were originally Jarrolds' prints as well, prints from the Cromer Museum collections and a few from other sources. We hope you enjoy this collection of views of Cromer and Overstrand, Sheringham and other places in East Anglia, that come into the Poppyland story.

Front Cover: Cromer West Beach c. 1890
Inside Front Cover: The Heart of Poppyland - The Garden of Sleep
Title Page: Edwardian Bathers
Overleaf: Cromer Beach, 1872
Opposite: Cromer Pier about 1910. *(D. J. Cleveland)*

Published by Poppyland Publishing, Cromer, Norfolk.
Designed, typeset and printed by Speedprint Design, Spalding, Lincs.
Line drawings by the Author.
First edition published 1983.
Reprinted 1988.

ISBN 0 946148 03 1

Contents

Chapter One
Before the Poppyland Invasion

1. View of Cromer, Norfolk. Frontispiece to "Cromer considered as a watering-place," by E. Bartell (1806). From the West Cliffs, showing Cromer's first lighthouse, built in 1719. This engraving testifies to Bartell's comment that it was very rare not to see any shipping off the coast of Cromer.

"Approaching within half a mile of the town with the lighthouse and the hills as a background .... makes altogether a picture where the sublime and the beautiful are equally blended." E. Bartell, 1806.

2. *(Inset)* **Fishermen's Cottages on the cliffs, Overstrand, by R. Dixon.** This drawing has been dated at 1810, when Overstrand was a village of 240 people, with a fishing-station on the beach called "Beck-Hythe."

"This amphitheatre is richly interspersed with cornfields, cottages and farm houses," presenting a scene of "pastoral simplicity." E. Bartell, 1806.

3. A South-East view of Cromer (1823) by J. Varley, engraved by W. Read. An interesting drawing, for it was made only one year after the jetty was built, showing the original Bath House on stilts that was situated on the beach and Webbs House on the cliff-top site of today's Watch House.

"The want of a large and well conducted inn is amongst those few things which are chiefly to be regretted by those who pay a visit to Cromer, but with the addition of such, Cromer would, perhaps, in the course of a few years, stand a chance of rivalling some of the more celebrated bathing-places." E. Bartell, 1806.

4. *(above left)* **East Beach, Cromer. (1850's).**
5. *(above right)* **Cromer from the Beach. (1850's).**

"True, indeed, it has not the metropolitan luxuries of Brighton, or the elegances of some of our more southern favourites, to recommend it; neither does it offer many resources of gaiety for the amusement of its visitors; but nevertheless, it will never want of admirers, so long as an unvitiated taste, a desire of scientific knowledge, or a wish for the renovation of health shall exist." "A Guide to Cromer by a Visitor," (1867).

6. *(left)* **Church Street looking towards the Albion Hotel (mid 19th century).** "The inhabitants, almost universally speaking, are extremely civil and well-behaved, respectable in themselves, and respectful towards others; simple in their manners and free from that spirit of extortion which is but commonly the fault of those who have only a short season to enable them to meet many exigencies and who only have a partial interest in those they serve." "A Guide to Cromer ...." (1867).

7. Cromer from the cliff path (1875-1886). A plea from Louise Hoare, who first visited Cromer in 1875 .... "I personally should like the tradition to continue of quiet Sundays, peaceful shore and seafront, where families can enjoy each other and their children . Give them good music, good acting and perhaps a place for teas and quiet. Let us keep Cromer somewhat as it has been." "Cromer Memories," L. Hoare.

8. *(above)* **East Beach, Cromer (1858-67).** Taken from the jetty, this early photograph shows the white-faced Bath House built by Simeon Simons on the Esplanade, which provided hot and cold sea-water baths for visitors and a newspaper subscription room.

9. *(below)* **The "Wensleydale" (1870).** One of the coal ships that served Cromer up until the 1870's and 1880's, owned by Mr. J. Cross and sold in 1879.

"The sea at Cromer, is almost always diversified by a change of moving objects; the trade from Newcastle, Sunderland and the Baltic keeping up a constant succession of vessels; to which may be added the regular appearance of the various steam-vessels which ply between London and the Northern parts." "A Guide to Cromer ...." (1867).

10. *(left)* **East Beach, Cromer (1869).** Two other Cromer coal ships, the "Commerce" and the "Ellis," or "Plumper" as it was sometimes nicknamed, on the beach. The recently completed lifeboat house can be seen on the left of the picture.

11. *(right)* **The View from Cromer High Station (1880's), by the Rev. Simpson.** An early 20th century newspaper comment ..."There was a time within the past twenty years when nearly every inhabitant depended for a living either on the harvest of the sea or that of the land. And a little farther back the grand old church tower might have cast its shadow upon all that there was of Cromer." "Daily Express."

12. *(below)* **Cromer High Station c.1900.** The author of "A Guide to Cromer ...." (1878) noted that, "Happily it (Cromer) is now accessible by railway, which from Norwich, passes through the beautiful village of Thorpe on the Yare, Wroxham, North Walsham and Gunton, where there is a fine station. On arriving at Cromer, the visitor, on alighting from the train, will have a commanding view of the ocean and the surrounding country."

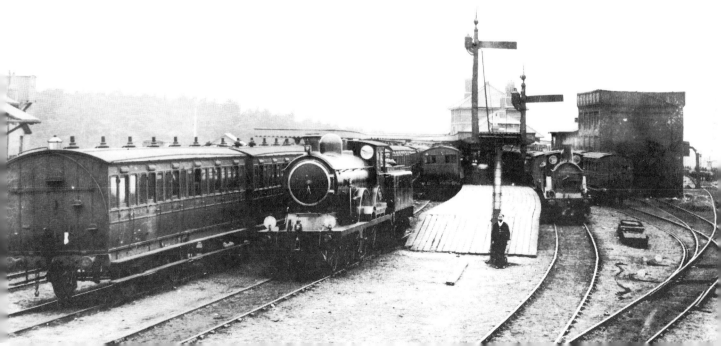

13. *(Top left)* **Cromer from the Cliff. (1881).** W. White, 1883 ...."Cromer is a fashionable bathing-place and well-built town, picturesquely seated on the lofty cliffs." "History, Gazetteer and Directory of Norfolk ...."

14. *(top right)* **General view from the West Cliffs (1881).** "The jetty is the fashionable resort of the evening, the company assembling here; some to enjoy the pure sea breezes, to watch the noble billows .... or the mild splendour of the moon; others to meet their acquaintances and a few, perhaps ... for the exercise of their satirical talents." "A Guide to Cromer ...." (1867).

15. *(left)* **Sheringham Beach, late 19th century.** "Sheringham .... comprises the villages of Upper and Lower Sheringham:- the latter, on the sea cliffs, is entirely a fishing place; and the former, more than a mile inland, is mainly agricultural." "White's Directory," (1883).

Chapter Two
The Arrival of Clement Scott

16. *(below left)* **Cromer Beach from the West Cliff (1888).** "Sand-life at Cromer is not like sand-life elsewhere. There is plenty of amusement, but very little noise." "Poppyland," C. Scott (1886).

"Custom had established a certain fashion at this pretty little watering-place and it was religiously obeyed; it was the rule to go on the sands in the morning, to walk on one cliff for a mile in the afternoon, to take another mile in the other direction at sunset and to crowd upon the little pier at night." "Poppyland," C. Scott (1886).

"The eye of the speculative builder is firmly fixed on poor little Cromer." "Poppyland," C. Scott (1886).

17. *(Below)* **East Cliffs, Cromer, c.1898.** "A veritable flower-garden." "Poppyland," C. Scott, (1886). Extract from "A Plea from Poppyland ....."
"Sing of our cliffs
　　that overlook the sand!
　Sing of our mother,
　　the green-girdled sea!

Sing of the light
　that lingers on the land!
Sing of the love that was
　and is to be!
　　"Lays and Lyrics," C. Scott (1888)

18. *(Left)* **The Cliffs, Cromer - looking towards East Runton.**
"The Cliffside Path"
"Seaward goes the sun,
　and homeward by the down
We, before the night
　upon his grave be sealed.
Low behind us lies the
　bright steep murmering town.
High before us
　heaves the steep rough silent field.
Breach by ghastlier breach,
　the cliffs collapsing yield:
Half the path is broken,
　half the banks divide;
Flawed and crumbled, riven and rent,
　they cleave and slide
Toward the ridged and wrinkled
　waste of girdling sand
Deep beneath, whose furrows tell
　how far and wide
Wind is lord and change
　is sovereign of the strand."
　　"A Midsummer Holiday .... "
　　Swinburne (1884)

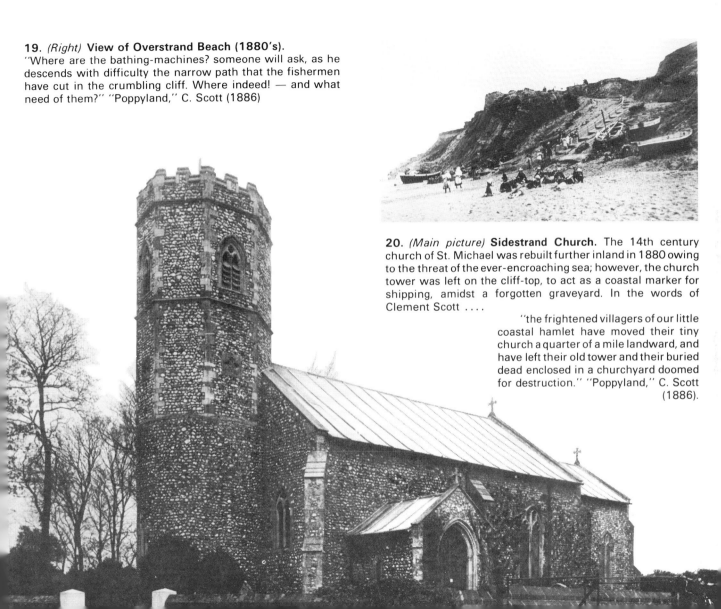

19. *(Right)* **View of Overstrand Beach (1880's).**
"Where are the bathing-machines? someone will ask, as he descends with difficulty the narrow path that the fishermen have cut in the crumbling cliff. Where indeed! — and what need of them?" "Poppyland," C. Scott (1886)

20. *(Main picture)* **Sidestrand Church.** The 14th century church of St. Michael was rebuilt further inland in 1880 owing to the threat of the ever-encroaching sea; however, the church tower was left on the cliff-top, to act as a coastal marker for shipping, amidst a forgotten graveyard. In the words of Clement Scott ....

"the frightened villagers of our little coastal hamlet have moved their tiny church a quarter of a mile landward, and have left their old tower and their buried dead enclosed in a churchyard doomed for destruction." "Poppyland," C. Scott (1886).

21. *(Left)* **Clement Scott, (1897).** Clement Scott, who by his pen immortalised "Poppyland," as reads the inscription on the memorial erected to the writer in 1909.

22. *(Right)* **Louie Jermy.** "The Maid of the Mill," to whom Scott dedicated his book "Poppyland" thus .... "To Louie Jermy, without whose kindliness, affection and sympathy, Poppyland, its peace and pleasures, would have been an unknown region and no paradise to Clement Scott."

23. The Mill House and Louie Jermy. First impressions of the miller's house from "Poppyland" ....

"It was one of those farmhouses which is an exact reproduction of the cottage that children are set to draw when they begin their first lesson. A little red-brick house with three white windows on the first floor, a little white door in the middle, a window at either side, and a stack of chimneys at each end of the cottage. The house was divided from the road by a white gate and palings, and in front of it was a garden, brilliant with flowers."

24. *(Above)* **The Garden of Sleep - An Artist's Impression, by P. W. Pocock.** (1880's).
25. *(Main picture)* **"Tower, Gate and Young Lady."**

"The Garden of Sleep" - Clement Scott
(subtitled "A Summer Song")

"On the grass of the cliff, at the edge of the steep,
  God planted a garden, a garden of sleep!
'Neath the blue of the sky, in the green of the corn,
  It is there that the royal red poppies are born!
  Brief days of desire, and long dreams of delight,
They are mine when my Poppyland cometh in sight.
  In music of distance, with eyes that are wet,
  It is there I remember, and there I forget!
O! heart of my heart! where the poppies are born,
  I am waiting for thee, in the hush of the corn.
    Sleep! Sleep!
   From the Cliff to the Deep!
    Sleep, my Poppy-land,
     Sleep!

In my garden of sleep, where red poppies are spread,
  I wait for the living, alone with the dead!
For a tower in ruins stands guard o'er the deep,
At whose feet are green graves of dear women asleep!
  Did they love, as I love, when they lived by the sea?
  Did they wait, as I wait, for the days that may be?
Was it hope or fulfilling, that entered each breast,
  Ere death gave release, and the poppies gave rest?
  O! life of my life! on the cliffs by the sea,
By the graves in the grass, I am waiting for thee!
    Sleep! Sleep!
   In the Dews by the Deep!
    Sleep, my Poppy-land,
     Sleep!"

Poppyland Visitors

26. *(Top centre)* **Swinburne and Watts-Dunton.** Described as "intimate friends," the two poets were both inspired by the beauties of the area. Watts-Dunton dedicated his book to his future wife, Clara, "In remembrance of Sunny Days and Starlit Nights, when we rambled together on crumbling cliffs that are now at the bottom of the sea. This edition of the story which has been a link between us IS INSCRIBED." Swinburne dedicated his book of poems "A Midsummer Holiday" simply, "To Theodore Watts."

27. *(Bottom centre)* **George Sims.**
"On one of his visits Sims rifled Louie's store-cupboard and packed all her bottled blackberries and bottles of blackberry jam away - so that none was available for Clement Scott when he arrived the next day - who then said, 'No puddings, Louie?' - 'Then no pay!' "Leaves from an Overstrand Scrapbook" (unpublished), compiled by G. Parry.

28. *(Top left)* **Henry Irving.**
29. *(Top right)* **Wilson Barrett.**
"Louie was particularly attracted to poets, authors and actors .... On rare occasions, she treated herself to a short London holiday to enjoy a melodrama at Drury Lane by Wilson Barrett, or a tragedy at the Lyceum with Henry Irving in the title role." "The Maid of the Mill," edited by G. Parry (1936)

Chapter Three
The Poppyland Image

31. *(Below)* **Cromer from the East. (1903).**

"A Haven" (extract)

.... "East and North a waste of waters, south and west
Lonelier lands than dreams in sleep would feign to be,
When the soul goes forth on travel, and is prest
Round and compassed in with clouds that flash and flee.
Dells without a streamlet, downs without a tree,
Cirques of hollow cliff that crumble, give their guest
Little hope, till hard at hand he pause, to see
Where the small town smiles, a warm still sea-side nest" ....
    "A Midsummer Holiday," Swinburne. (1884)

30. *(Above)* **Golfing, by Parsons Norman.** The Royal Cromer Golf Course was opened in 1895, it must have proved a great attraction, for in "The Lady" in 1914, Cromer was hailed to be, "one of the most delightful of golfing resorts."

30 - 36 *(Following pages)* **A selection of postcards showing the various ways in which the image was used, and abused even, in order to attract visitors ....**

22

32. West Runton from the Roman Camp. In his "Poppyland" Scott wrote of the "Exmoor-like scenery at Beeston, where on an eminence said to be a Roman encampment, but more probably an old beacon station, may be viewed the fairest prospect of distant sea and near foliage that ever delighted the picturesque sense."

33 & 34. The Garden of Sleep. On every New Year's Eve for fifteen years Scott is said to have walked along Tower Lane and spent the last few moments of the old year on the cliffs in his "Garden of Sleep."

"The Old Church Tower" (extract)
"In such a place to ponder,
Two hearts when looking yonder,
might falter or grow fonder
 Than other hearts have been.
But picture it, and tell me,
If any harm befell me,
What place of peace should knell me
 To dreams in worlds unseen.

One night can you remember,
The last of white December,
When love relit the ember
 That time was burning low;
Once more in soul united,
The moon above us lighted
The tower where we plighted
 Our faith of long ago.

Oh! sad forgotten tower!
Thou hast the peace and power,
To tell the storms that shower
 Across thy sister sea.
Look downward, and behold us:
What mysteries infold us,
Thou promised love, and told us
 The present - and to be."
 "Lays and Lyrics," C. Scott (1888)

35. (Left) Miller Jermy, Overstrand.

"The Mill Garden" (extract)
"Stately stand the sunflowers, glowing down
    the garden-side,
Ranged in royal rank a row along
    the warm grey wall,
Whence their deep disks burn at rich midnoon
    afire with pride,
Even as though their beams indeed were sunbeams,
    and the tall
Sceptral stems bore stars whose reign endures not
    flowers that fall.
Lowlier laughs and basks the kindlier flower
    of homelier fame.
Held by love the sweeter that it blooms in
    Shakespeare's name,
Fragrant yet as though his hand had touched and
    made it thrill,
Like the whole world's heart, with warm new life
    and gladdening flame.
Fair befall the fair green close that lies
    below the mill!"
        "A Midsummer Holiday," Swinburne. (1884)

36. (Right) The Miller's Cottage, Overstrand. "Poppyland Cottage."

"A Plea from Poppyland" (extract)
.... "Sing of immortal love! inhabiting
Our rose-girt cottage shadowed by the mill;
Go forth into our moonlight once, and sing
Of life, of love, of God's triumphant will!" ....
        "Lays and Lyrics," C. Scott. (1888)

37. *(Above)* **Poppyland Bouquet.** The letter reads .... "The Marchioness of .... is pleased to tell Mr. Davidson that she finds his Poppyland Bouquet a most delicious perfume."

Poppyland china was produced by local firms such as Jarrolds, Rounce and Wortley, and B. A. Watts of Sheringham. It was made in Staffordshire, and sold locally. The perfume "Poppyland Bouquet" was made by Daniel Davison of Cromer, and sold all over the World between 1890 and 1930.

38. *(Opposite)* **Jarrolds' poster of Cromer.**

'"Cromer Cliffs" (extract)
.... "Here on my back in the sunshine lying
On the Lighthouse cliffs amidst flowers and grass,
I dreamily stir when the swallow is flying,
and lazily listen when travellers pass" ....
"Lays and Lyrics," C. Scott. (1888)

PRICE. 1/6.

VERA IN POPPYLAND

ILLUSTRATED BY WALTER W. RUSSELL

JARROLD. & SONS. 3. PATERNOSTER BUILDINGS. E.C.

39. *(Above)* **The cover of "Vera in Poppyland." Mrs. A. Berlyn. (1893-5).**
"To my friend Clement Scott, the discoverer of "Poppyland," whose charming papers first led my steps to that peaceful haven, this little book is gratefully inscribed." Mrs. A. Berlyn.

CROMER

FOR ILLUSTRATED GUIDE - APPLY. CLERK. DISTRICT COUNCIL. (POSTAGE 1ᵈ)

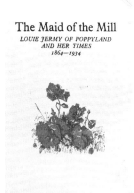

The Maid of the Mill

LOUIE JERMY OF POPPYLAND
AND HER TIMES
1864-1934

40. *(Right)* **Sketch from ''Vera in Poppyland,''** More symptoms of ''Scotto-mania'' ....

''Sylvia has already lost her heart to an unknown hero, at whose shrine, the little white-gated mill-house up the road, she has come prepared to make oblations of poppies, and chant his own sweet hymn to the dead who lie at rest 'at the edge of the steep.' '' ''Vera in Poppyland,'' Mrs. A. Berlyn. (1893-5)

41. *(Centre)* **Sketch from ''Vera in Poppyland.''**

''beneath us the sea beat fiercely against the cliffs, almost dashing its spray to our feet, and hungrily struggling as it were,

to grasp the sleeping dead from their grassy beds among the poppies.'' ''Vera in Poppyland,'' Mrs. A. Berlyn. (1893-5)

42. *(Top left)* **The cover of ''The Maid of the Mill,'' edited by G. Parry. (1936).** Extract from the foreword ....

''Louie Jermy was unconsciously

responsible for the changes that came and with them for the subsequent prosperity of the village (Overstrand) and the pleasure it has since given to thousands of visitors. Such changes are regretted by those who joy in the wide open spaces .... and prefer peace to pylons and all they imply.''

43. *(Bottom left)* **The cover of the fourth edition of ''Poppyland,'' C. Scott. (1899).** Ruskin ''On Poppies,'' used by Scott as a preface to his book ....

''Wherever men are noble they love bright colour: and wherever they can live healthily, bright colour is given them in sky, sea, flowers, and living creatures!''

Chapter Four
'The Village of Millionaires.'

44 - 48 *(Following pages)* **"The Pleasaunce," Overstrand**

44. *(Below)* **"The Pleasaunce," West Front, 1904.**
45. *(Left)* **The Italian Garden.**

"Cyril Flower's red cliff-side cottage, with its pretty verandah, its garden of poppies, has great fascination." Clement Scott

A certain amount of the credit for the building boom in Overstrand in the late 1880's and 1890's must go to the influence and example of Lord and Lady Battersea. In 1888 Cyril Flower M.P., Lord Battersea, bought two adjoining properties in the village on the advice of Lord Suffield. The M.P. and his wife, Constance de Rothschild, had previously enjoyed annual holidays on the East coast of Norfolk. Under the guidance of Lord Battersea and the skill of the architect Sir Edwin Lutyens, "The Cottage," or "The Pleasaunce" as it was renamed, underwent considerable alteration and rebuilding.

46. *(Above)* **The Cloisters.**
47. *(Left)* **The Water Garden.**

In 1889 Princess Louise is said to have stayed at the house almost unnoticed. Scott wrote that she "took her tea on the wee lawns and nobody ever turned their heads to look at her." Other notable visitors to "The Pleasaunce" were George Meredith, Lord Morely, and Sir Sidney Lee.

The grounds of the house were named "The Garden of Dreams," in opposition to the "Garden of Sleep," an idea said to have been taken from a novel by the Hon. Mrs. Felkin entitled "Ten Degrees Backward."

48. Interior, showing Japanese curios.

49. *(Main picture)* **Overstrand, main street, 1904.**
50. *(Inset)* **The Danish Pavilion, 1904.**

Writing of the houses in Overstrand during the summer season, Lady Battersea, in her book "Reminiscences," stated that, "it would be difficult to find the owners of these houses at home in them, for the premises are systematically let to the numerous seaside visitors who have had the good sense to discover the charm of the place, which, without the ordinary attractions such as a pier, a band, and shows of all sorts, can hold its own with many a popular coast resort."

The Danish House, or Pavilion, was purchased by Sir George Henry Lewis, a banker and lawyer, from an exhibition in Paris, and constructed on land he bought in the village in the late 19th century.

51. *(Left)* **Overstrand Hall, 1904.** The Hall was built originally for Lord and Lady Hillingdon, and was designed by Lutyens. Today it is the Leicester Convalescent Home.

52. *(Right)* **Seamarge, 1904.**
"Sir Edgar Speyer, with his wealth and taste, was a modern Lorenzo di Medici, and in his happier, earlier days he chose Overstrand for his country seat, on the same Norfolk coast where Royal Sandringham is situated. Regardless of cost he erected at Overstrand from the finest authentic Elizabethan oak, brick and tile, a splendid house, designed by the late Arthur Bloomfield R.I.B.A. The gardens were ornamented with Italian sculpture." "Leaves from an Overstrand Scrapbook" (unpublished), G. Parry.

At the beginning of World War One, however, Sir Edgar was removed from his post as Privy Councillor and deported, owing to his German origin.

53 & 54. The Overstrand Hotel. This building is described in Gwen Parry's scrapbook as ....
"A leading hotel which recaptured the wealth of the earlier period for some twenty years." Built towards the close of the 19th century, later the victim of cliff falls, it was eventually demolished.

55. *(Left)* **Overstrand Church, 1880's.**
56. *(Above)* **Overstrand Churches.**

In 1859 it was decided that the 14th century church of St. Martin was in need of restoration, but instead, a new church was built beside it, Christchurch, opened in 1867. By 1911, however, this building was no longer large enough for its increasing congregation, and St. Martin's was therefore restored and reopened in 1914.

57. Overstrand.

"Overstrand is a spot wherein noise seems always out of place. Its perfect peace, its absolute restfulness, its inexpressible calm .... the unspeakable repose of the land covers one as with a soft fleecy garment, and to leave undisturbed the stillness and the beauty around seems the most fitting way of all to enjoy sweet Poppyland." "Vera in Poppyland," Mrs. A. Berlyn. (1893-5)

58. *(Left)* **Overstrand from the Cromer road, 1890's.**
59. *(Below left)* **Overstrand from the Links. 60.** *(Below right)* **Overstrand from the Mill.**

"Overstrand is a charming combination of green fields, blue sea, and rugged cliffs, and has a great future before it. I strongly recommend anyone who wants perfect rest and glorious air amid beautiful scenery to try Overstrand." "The Maid of the Mill," edited by G. Parry (1936).

61. *(Right)* **Promenade, Overstrand, early 20th century.**
62. *(Above)* **Overstrand Beach, early 20th century.**
63. *(Next page)* **Overstrand Beach, c.1920.**

Observation from a newspaper, 1901....
"It is the exhilaration which comes from climbing the successively rising cliffs by the sea that provides the charm of it all .... what a joy to be away from the stifling strand with its noise and rush and din. There is a special sanctity about this clean, exhuberant spot."

Chapter Five
A Building Boom

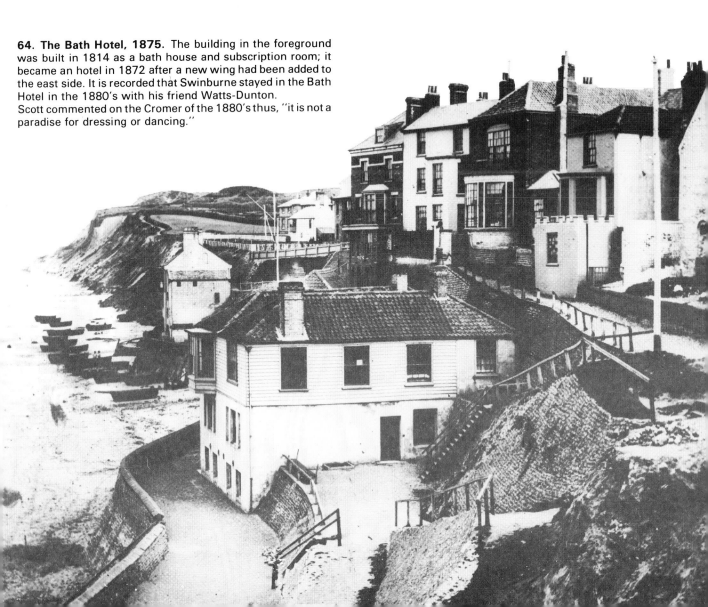

64. The Bath Hotel, 1875. The building in the foreground was built in 1814 as a bath house and subscription room; it became an hotel in 1872 after a new wing had been added to the east side. It is recorded that Swinburne stayed in the Bath Hotel in the 1880's with his friend Watts-Dunton.

Scott commented on the Cromer of the 1880's thus, "it is not a paradise for dressing or dancing."

65. *(Above)* **The Marlborough Hotel (1890's).**
66. *(Right)* **Marlborough Hotel, Cromer (early 20th century).**

Built in stages between 1883 and 1889, this hotel began as a small boarding house. Originally it was built for Mrs. S. Rogers but was later extended by her son, Mr. F. W. Rogers, who is reputed to have been the first car-owner in Cromer. The hotel stood on the corner of Prince of Wales road until it was demolished in the 1950's.

67. *(Right)* **Cromer Church during restoration (1885).**
68. *(Below)* **Cromer Church (c.1900).**

"The old grey flint church and its solemn old grey tower with a speculative estate." "Poppyland," C. Scott (1886).

In 1871 and 1873 Cromer's church tower had been badly damaged by lightning, consequently repairs had to be carried out in 1885-6. The tower was restored at a cost of £1,365 and the chancel was re-built on its original foundations at a cost of £7,861, the architect being Sir A. Bloomfield.

69. The Royal Cromer Hotel, Newhaven Court. Newhaven Court was originally built as a private residence for the Lampson family in 1885. Many distinguished visitors stayed there as guests, including Oscar Wilde, Tennyson, and Churchill. The owner's second wife, Jane, was said to have been mainly responsible for the building of this residence, and under a photograph of the house Locker Lampson wrote . . . .

"This is the house by Cromer town,
Its bricks are red, they look so brown
It faces the sea on a wind-swept hill -
In Winter its empty; in Summer its chill.
Indeed it is one of Earth's spots
As we know from the smashing of chimney pots,
In August I ask for an extra quilt
This is the house that Jane built."

45

70. A rehearsal for 'King Canute.' Commander Oliver Locker Lampson rehearsing 'King Canute' for a carnival. From left to right: Locker Lampson, the King of Greece, Mrs. Locker Lampson, Princess Illeana, Sir W. Bull M.P.

71. Royal Cromer Hotel. When Oliver Locker Lampson inherited the house from his father in 1915 he turned it into an hotel which acquired a world-wide reputation, and was patronised by many members of the European royal families.

72. *(Right)* **Red Lion Steps, Promenade, and Jetty. (1894-97).**
73. *(Below)* **East Beach, (1901).**

"that red-roofed village, the centre of all that was fashionable and select." "Poppyland," C. Scott (1886).

In 1887 a new Red Lion Hotel was built for Mr. John Smith of London, on the same site as an older hotel of the same name. Mr. Smith also bought other property in Cromer in the same era.

The new Promenade and the eastern section of the sea wall had been constructed in 1894 by the town's Protection Commissioners.

74. The Metropole Hotel. This hotel was built in 1893 and stands on the site of the late 18th century merchant's storage building known as Ditchell's Barn. The hotel was one of several used by troops in Cromer during World War Two.

75. *(Left)* **Drawing for the new Town Hall, Cromer.**
76. *(Below left)* **The Town Hall in 1890.**
77. *(Below right)* **Programme of entertainment, 1909.**

"The nigger and the music-hall minstrel never desert Yarmouth for its quieter neighbour." One of Clement Scott's less prophetic statements concerning Cromer. "Poppyland" (1886).

Opened in 1890, the Town Hall was designed by the architect George Skipper of Norwich, who was also responsible for designing several hotels in Cromer in the late 19th century. The building became known as the Town Hall Theatre, and today it is a warehouse.

Cromer Post Office

Minstrel Entertainment,
TOWN HALL, CROMER,
Wednesday, February 10th, 1909

Interlocutor:
C. H. WHITE.

Bones: Tambo:
W. H. BALLS.   A. W. LOVICK.

Pianist: JACK WHITE

SAUL SALKIND,
For GOLD and SILVER JEWELLERY
ARTISTIC and UP TO DATE
SILVER & ELECTRO PLATED GOODS
SUITABLE FOR PRESENTATION
Best House for
WEDDING and ENGAGEMENT RINGS
Church Street, Cromer.

78. *(Opposite)* **Cromer from the east, c.1910.**
79. *(Left)* **Cover of the sale catalogue of the Cromer Hall Estate (1891).**
80. *(Above)* **The Grand Hotel, Cromer (1895-6).**

In 1890, as a result of the building of the new Beach Station, Mr. B. Bond Cabbell of Cromer Hall announced the forthcoming sale of a portion of land on Cromer's West Cliffs. As an added attraction to buyers, it was also announced that a "Grand Hotel" was to be built there. A group of businessmen were responsible for financing the hotel; it was designed by Skipper, and furnished by Trevor Page Limited of Norwich. Once this hotel had been completed more land was put on sale in 1891 and additional hotels were built in this area of the town. 51

82. *(Left)* **The Cliftonville Hotel (early 20th century).** The Cliftonville Hotel was re-built in 1894 for Wiliam Churchyard of Westbourne House, West Street, who owned a row of shops and a boarding house there.

The "Daily Telegraph" 1901 . . . . "Cromer, when you get into it, wears the red-brick badge of modern sea-shore prosperity . . . . Altogether, the evidence of Cromer's health and good fortune is almost aggressive. But there is a refreshing irregularity on its seafront, uncommon in most of the prosperous seaside resorts."

81. *(Below)* **Cromer from the West (1899).** This photograph was taken after the West Parade Hotel had been built next to the Grand.

83. *(Above)* **Pier Head (1901-03).**
84. *(Below)* **Cromer Pier.**

The new pier was built in 1901, and was opened on the 8th June of that year. The engineers were Douglas and Arnott of London. A bandstand was built on the end of the new pier, but it was replaced with a pavilion for a theatre in 1905.

85. The Pier, Cromer (1920's).

86. North Lodge, Overstrand road. (c.1910). Originally the property of the Goldsmith Company, in 1857 this building became the private summer residence of Joseph Hoare, the eldest son of Samuel and Louisa Hoare of Cliff House. In 1886 a new wing was added, and the house continued to be a summer residence of the Hoare family until 1928, when it was bought by Cromer Council.

87. The Fletcher. (early 20th century). The Fletcher was built in 1892 by B. E. Fletcher Esq. of Marlingford Hall. The plans for the building were drawn up by Mr. E. Boardman of Norwich. It was built originally as a seaside convalescent home for patients from the Norfolk and Norwich Hospital, but eventually became the property of Cromer Hospital.

Dear Gladys
I hope you are enjoying your stay at Thorpe. We are having nice times at Cromer. There are lovely sands at Lowtide.

With Love from man.

CROMER. HOTEL DE PARIS.

88. *(Top left)* **From the Jetty (1890).**
89. *(Above)* **The Hotel de Paris, Opening Day, 1895.**
90. *(Left)* **Postcard of the Hotel de Paris.**

The original Hotel de Paris opened as a boarding house in the 1830's, but was already listed as an hotel by 1845. This building had previously been called "Marine Villa," and was the summer residence of Lord Suffield, from whom Pierre le François purchased it in 1830. George Skipper was commissioned to re-design the hotel in 1894, incorporating Albert House next door and a part of the Belle Vue Hotel.

91. *(Left)* **Royal Links Hotel, Cromer.** As a result of the success of the Royal Cromer Golf Club it was decided that an hotel was needed to accommodate the many distinguished visitors. The Links Hotel was therefore built in 1895, under the joint initiative of Lord Suffield and Henry Broadhurst M.P., its first patron being H.R.H. the Prince of Wales, later Edward VII. Mysteriously, the hotel was destroyed by fire in the 1940's.

"A castle of indolence on the topmost height of a sea-kissed down." Clement Scott.

92. *(Right)* **The Sheringham Hotel, built in 1889.** A newspaper comment of 1901 .... "Sheringham has ceased to be the odiferous, dirty little refuse-heap of decaying fish which led some of us to satirise its 'attractions' a few years ago. It is a bright little seaside resort, striving valiantly to do justice to the perpetual delights of its unrivalled environment and its beauteous scenery."

Chapter Six
Poppyland Holidays

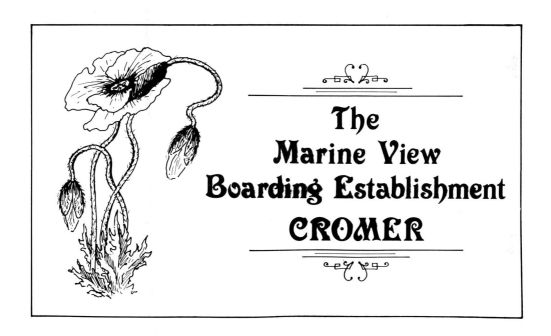

The
Marine View
Boarding Establishment
CROMER

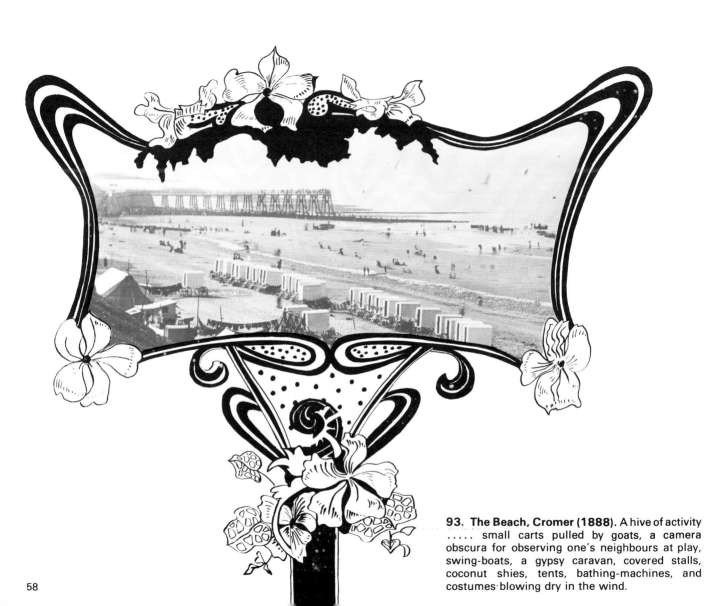

93. The Beach, Cromer (1888). A hive of activity ..... small carts pulled by goats, a camera obscura for observing one's neighbours at play, swing-boats, a gypsy caravan, covered stalls, coconut shies, tents, bathing-machines, and costumes blowing dry in the wind.

94. Cromer Sands, "After the last bathe" (1892). Seaside Sketches ..... Cromer and its Crabs - "Daily News" 1904 .... "For robust mortals wishful to be even more robust, Cromer is the place ..... Your lungs are strengthened by air blowing pure and unadulterated from the North Pole ... It is on the fringe of Poppyland - a region of fairy prettiness; and the Cromer sunshine will bring out all your freckles ..... G.E.R. expresses cover the 139 miles from Liverpool Street in less than three hours ..... Cromer, with its perfect sands, is famous for its bathing."

95. *(Above)* **Cromer Beach (1898).**
96. *(Right)* **The Beach, Cromer (1892).**

The sight of local fishermen taking visitors for trips in their boats was a common one in the 1890's, they even carried the ladies out to the boats to ensure that their dresses and feet did not get wet.

Fishermen's Lore ..... "If the clouds are gathering thick and fast, keep sharp lookout for sail and mast, but if they slowly onward crawl, shoot your nets, lines and trawl."

"The evening red and morning grey, are sure signs of a fine day, but, the evening grey and morning red, makes the fisherman shake his head."

"A rainbow in the morning, is the fisherman's warning, a rainbow at night, is the sailor's delight."

97. *(Inset)* **Cromer Beach (1898).**
98. **East Beach, Cromer from the Steps. (1898).**

"Paddling, I need scarcely observe, consists of skirting the fringe or margin of the sea with naked feet, and the pleasure is derived from the wavelets at low tide breaking upon the lower extremities, relieved from the encumbrance of shoes and stockings." "Poppyland," C. Scott (1886).
"The children at Cromer, so far as I have observed, are all good children." "Poppyland," C. Scott (1886).

99. East Beach from the Gangway (1890's).
100. Bathing Regulations (1898).

The "Cromer and North Walsham Post," 1892 .... "A fortnight ago we drew attention to the want that existed on the part of some of the bathers at Cromer of that sense of decency which is supposed to be innate in civilised human beings. We are sorry it is necessary to refer to the subject again ... Unfortunately, the nuisance has not yet been stopped, and we have been urged both by visitors and residents to raise a protest against the bathing of men and women within the same area."

101. East Beach, Cromer (c.1897) "In those days bathing machines were pulled into the sea by a horse, generally ridden by a small boy. The bathers stepped down the ladder into the sea clothed from neck to knee in blue bathing gowns trimmed with scarlet tape. There was no mixed bathing then." "Cromer Memories," L. Hoare.

102. East Beach, Cromer (1895).
Clement Scott described the scene on
Cromer beach when he first visited the
area .... ''There they all were, digging
on the sands, playing lawn tennis,
working, reading, flirting, and donkey-
riding.''

103. East Beach, Cromer on Regatta Day (1898). Cromer's Regatta was held annually, usually in August, there were sailing races for various types of vessel, and the lifeboat was used as a launch for the referee. Betting often took place over the races, and there was a pig hunt, a 'climbing the greasy pole competition,' and plenty of running and jumping contests for the children.

Sincere Greetings

104. Cromer Beach, Regatta Day (1898). Extract from a poem entitled ''Cromer Regatta; or Peter Clawpork's lament for the decline of field sports,'' composed by ''Old Tubby,'' early 19th century . . . .
"The day arrives, old farmer's wives,
with darters, Poll and Betty,
And bumpkin Tom, all eager come,
And prance on Cromer jetty;
While there they stand, some boats are man'd
Some thousand tongues all chatter,
Zounds, in my life, ne'er was such a strife, -
And this is the Regatta.''

105. Regatta Day, 1903. The launching of the ''Louisa Heartwell'' lifeboat on Regatta Day, accompanied by the coastguards in extra boats.

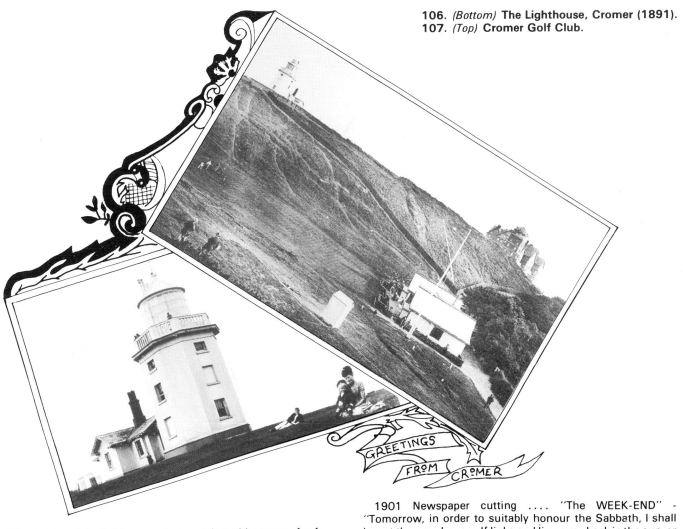

GREETINGS FROM CROMER

"The bright white lighthouse, that stands amidst acres of soft velvety turf and yellow sea-daisies" "Poppyland," C. Scott (1886)

1901 Newspaper cutting .... "The WEEK-END" - "Tomorrow, in order to suitably honour the Sabbath, I shall haunt the wondrous golf links and lie on my back in the sun, or dream through the summer hours in some secluded dell behind the lighthouse."

108. *(Left)* **Jarrolds' Frontage.**
109. *(Bottom right)* **Munday's Library.**
110. *(Top)* **Cromer from the West (1888).**

Greetings From~

CROMER

"It is a far cry from Skegness to Cromer. The aristocratic watering-place of East Anglia." "Everyman" Health and Holiday Resorts series, 1914.

In the evenings, "on the eastern cliff, all who would enjoy a peaceful scene are found walking at the cliff's edge towards Sheringham," "Poppyland," C. Scott (1886)

113. *(Top)* **Cromer from the East Cliff (1898)**

- One of the special Children's Services that were sometimes held on the cliff-tops.

Sundays were always observed very strictly, there was no beach, no paddling and no games. The children had to be dressed in their Sunday best clothes in order to attend church in the morning and to walk on the promenade in the afternoon.

111. *(Bottom left)* **Cromer from the East (c. 1902)**
112. *(Bottom right)* **A Sunday Morning Stroll (c.1902)**

69

114. *(Right)* **The Bandstand on the Pier (1901-1905).**
115. *(Left)* **Postcard of the Pier and Parade, looking east.**

Bands such as the Blue Viennese Band often played for the entertainment of the visitors.

"music and laughter and seaside merriment, from bands and bathing-machines, from crochet and circulating libraries." "Poppyland," C. Scott (1886)

116. Cromer Fishermen, c.1902. "At the corner of every street is a bronzed and healthy-faced sailor with a knowing look on his face which implies that it is the best possible day for a sail or a fishing expedition." "Poppyland," C. Scott (1886)

117. The "Louisa Heartwell" and Crew, Launching Day, 1902.
118. Henry Blogg (photo by Olive Edis).

The "Louisa Heartwell," 1902-1932, was built by the Thames Ironwork Company at a cost of £982. She was named thus after the mother of Miss Emily Heartwell who met the cost of the boat with her legacy. The lifeboat was sold in 1932 for only £55. Her Cox'n from 1909 was Henry Blogg, the most decorated of all lifeboatmen.

"Henry was a very downright man. I remember introducing a relation to him who thought that she knew him very well. He shook hands politely but said, I'm sure, Madam, I don't remember you: I've never seen you before' - rather daunting for my friend!" "Cromer Memories," L. Hoare.

"He was a very humble man and hated to be praised. The George Cross and other medals were put away in a cardboard box and seldom shown to anyone." "Cromer Memories," L. Hoare.

Chapter Seven
Poppyland Farther Afield

119. *(Top)* **Sheringham High Street.**
120. *(Bottom)* **Sheringham Beach 1895.**

In 1906 the author of an article about Sheringham wrote ....
"I would have you share in my joy in the strip of Norfolk coast on what has hitherto been called the wrong side of Cromer .... Sheringham, the friendly rival of Overstrand, is bent upon proving there is no wrong side of Cromer at all.'
"A New Seaside Resort."

121. The Beach, Mundesley-on-Sea. "North Devon Journal" 1905 - "Rambles in Poppyland" .... "Mundesley has beautiful sands, and in the summer a vast array of bathing-tents may be found there. Across these pleasant sands during the later years of his life, the poet Cowper took many a walk, resting his depressed spirit in the midst of soft sea breezes and the quiet music of the mid-summer sea."

122. *(Next page)* **Market-Place, Great Yarmouth.** "Yarmouth is the Blackpool of the Eastern Counties." "Sheffield Independent," 1914.

123. *(Right)* **The Jetty, Great Yarmouth.**
124. *(Below)* **The Beach, Great Yarmouth.**

"There is something irresistibly Dutch about this popular watering-place .... one of the most marvellous playgrounds of sand that I have ever found round and about these islands of ours." "Poppyland," C. Scott (1886)

"Yarmouth, as at present constituted is the veritable home of music-hall minstrelry," it is "a playground for the people." "Poppyland," C. Scott (1886).

125. *(Opposite)* **Lowestoft Harbour, early 20th century.**
126. *(This page)* **Lowestoft, early 20th century.**

127. The Beach, Lowestoft, early 20th century.

Scott wrote a chapter entitled "Lazy Lowestoft" in his "Poppyland" book, in which he described the town as being, "the very pink of propriety." He went on to describe the "trim and bandbox appearance of breezy Lowestoft," thus, "It is certainly the cleanest, neatest, and most orderly seaside spot at which I have ever cast anchor. There is an air of respectability at the very railway station, no confusion, no touting, no harassing, and no fuss.

128. *(Left)* **East Runton (1892).**
129. *(Below)* **The Sands, East Runton.**

Half the fun was getting thoroughly wet and untidy, jumping about from stone to stone and often slipping into the little pools." "Cromer Memories," L. Hoare.

"The Runton roads had cliffs and fields on either side. That part of the country was filled with wild flowers, some very rare Vipers Bugloss turns the cliff-top blue." "Cromer Memories," L. Hoare.

130. *(Below)* **Runton Gap.**
131. *(Right)* **East Runton Beach.**

132. *(Above)* **West Runton.**
133. *(Right)* **The Beach, West Runton.**

In Scott's opinion nothing could have ruined the peace of his Poppyland, ''the undisturbed quiet of such a spot that has the cleanliness of Cornwall .... and the air so pure, so bracing, so energising, and so health-giving.''

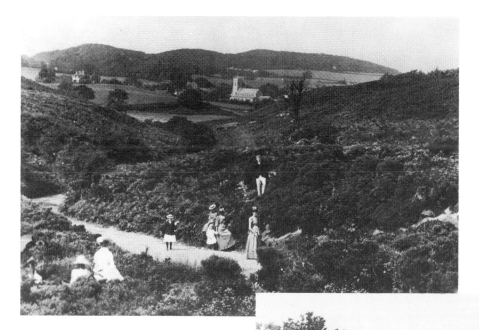

134. *(Above)* **Pretty Corner.**
135. *(Right)* **Roman Camp, near Cromer.**

"Our greatest treat was the donkey drives to the Black Beacon. Ben Kettle had several wicker chaises, of which we hired as many as we could. With one donkey boy between us we drove at snail's pace for two miles there. Then wild games of hide-and-seek amongst the trees and heather, with beautiful views over West Runton, Beeston and Sheringham." "Cromer Memories," L. Hoare.

136 & 137. The Lion's Mouth, Cromer

"At Felbrigg or Sheringham the heather blooms and the beeches wave, and the lovely silver pine, with its greenish-blue tassels, sighs all day in an air that braces nerve and sinew by its strength and softness." "Poppyland," C. Scott (1886).

138 & 139. *(Inset)* **The Lion's Mouth.**
"a country containing almost every possible variety of English scenery .... heather-covered heaths and commons .... lanes and roads, bordered on either side by thicket and wood, full of ground game and singing birds and playing places for the lively squirrel." "Poppyland," C. Scott (1886).

140. The Hut, Sheringham Woods. One of Clement Scott's "flower-fringed lanes."

141. *(Above)* **Northrepps Avenue.** The 1930 edition of the "Ward Lock Guide to Cromer and District" describes the area thus, "The country becomes well-wooded, an avenue affording pleasant shade for more than half a mile in the direction of Felbrigg woods .... The prospect is very pleasing."

142. *(Below)* **Northrepps Cottage.** Northrepps Cottage, built by Bartlett Gurney in 1793, was the birthplace of Elizabeth Fry, and the home of Anna Gurney.

143. *(Above)* **Beeches, Felbrigg Woods.** "North Devon Journal" 1905 - "Rambles in Poppyland" ....
"Among the trees are a number of beeches, and these have short thick trunks from which the branches spring at a short distance from the ground. This gives them a singular appearance, and one can easily understand the reason for the local name - 'The Lion's Mouth.' "

144. *(Below)* **Mustard Pot Lodge, Felbrigg.** The Lodge to Felbrigg Hall, a Tudor mansion, the home of the Felbrigges and the Windham family.

145. Picnic in Felbrigg Woods (1892). A favourite spot for picnics, with cakes from Breese's High Street shop to eat, cushions from a hired carriage to sit on, what better way to end a holiday in Poppyland?

Chapter Eight
The Demise of Poppyland?

146. *(Above)* **West Beach, Cromer (1920's).** "Holidays for Health and Pleasure," a newspaper article of 1924 …. "Fortunately, in our lovely little island home, tastes of all kinds are catered for. The large and fashionable seaside resorts - Scarborough, Cromer, and many others, are ever attractive to those who wish to mingle gaiety with the most bracing of sea breezes."

147. *(Below)* **Pier and Promenade, Cromer (1920's).**
148. *(Above)* **The Beach, Cromer (1920's).**

"Why you should come to Cromer," 1923 …"Cromer is Norfolk's select resort, there are no blatant, noisy distractions so common at many popular resorts, and the beach and promenades are entirely free from hawkers and touts. There are, however, no petty restrictions, and bathing is safe, and thoroughly enjoyable."

"Where to go on Holiday" - "Westminster Gazette" 1923 . . . .
(Poppyland) "to the north Cromer stands as the metropolis of Poppyland, no more appropriate phrase could have been coined to describe this pleasantly situated resort perched on dwarf cliffs, with its background of hilly woodlands aflame with the scarlet flower of the poppy" . . . .

. . . . "it would be a mistake to suppose that Cromer takes itself too seriously."

149. *(Above)* **West Beach, Cromer (1920's).**
150. *(Below)* **Beach and Promenade (1920's).**

Ye Olde Rocket House
Tea Gardens.
East Cliff, Cromer.

Pleasantly situated on Sea Front,
near Coastguard Station. - - -

✗ PUTTING GREEN. ✗

Light Luncheons and
Teas a Speciality.

HOME-MADE CAKES, SCONES AND CREAM ICES.

Orchestral Selections ... .. **4 to 6**
Dancing Every Evening ... ... **8 to 11**

Palmist in Attendance Daily.

Approach by Old Lifeboat Gangway,
Church Street, and Esplanade.

151. *(Opposite, far left)* **Jetty Street, Cromer (1920's).**
152. *(Above)* **Putting Greens (1920's).**
153. *(Right)* **Rocket House Gardens.**
154. *(Opposite right)* **Advertisement for the Rocket House Tea Rooms.**

In 1923 the "Birmingham Post" attributed Poppyland's popularity to its sunshine, sea breezes, golf, tennis, bands, pier, bathing, and boat trips.
1914 guide book .... "Cromer itself is exceedingly picturesque .... its quaint old streets widening into spacious avenues bordered by fine hotels, boarding houses, and charming well-built bungalows."

Cromer now has four putting greens in North Lodge Park, one on the West Cliff with a crazy golf course and a pitch and putt course on the Meadow.

155. *(Left)* **Sketch from Life, Louie Jermy, 1933.**
156. *(Below left)* **Louie Jermy's cottage, 1938.**
157. *(Below right)* **The Clement Scott Memorial.**
Remaining features of the Poppyland story in the 1930's.

Clement Scott died in 1904 and the old tower at Sidestrand had fallen over the cliffs in 1916. The Clement Scott memorial stands at the entrance to Poppyland, on the road between Cromer and Overstrand. Louie Jermy survived until 1934, having been evicted from her beloved Poppyland Cottage in 1919 and moved to a cottage in Tower Lane.

"The lane ended at the Garden of Sleep, immortalised by Clement Scott, and perhaps no more appropriate spot could have been found for her final retreat. The little rooms and the outhouse bristled with unplaced and unsorted belongings .... and I wondered how on earth she was ever going to accommodate them and produce order out of chaos." "The Maid of the Mill," edited by G. Parry (1936).

TO CLEMENT SCOTT, WHO BY HIS PEN IMMORTALISED "POPPYLAND" ERECTED BY MANY FRIENDS NOVEMBER 1909.

158. *(Above)* **West Beach and Promenade (1920's).**
159. *(Above right)* **Cromer from the East (1934).**

1943 official guide book ....
"snuggling comfortably in a pretty valley and bounded on three sides by some of Norfolk's finest scenery, Cromer is a happy and restful health resort well deserving of its bestowed title - 'Gem of the Norfolk Coast.' "

160. *(Right)* **Cromer, West Beach (1925).** "Cromer does not conform to any standard style or pattern - it is a resort which caters for every type of holidaymaker" "Guide to Cromer" 1943.

161. *(Above left)* **West Beach and Runton road (1950's).**
162. *(Above)* **Cromer from the West (1950's).**

1952 official guide book .... "This Norfolk Health Resort, with its quaint narrow streets, has a charm which is all its own, having preserved much of its natural appeal against a background of modern development."

163. *(Left)* **Tea Rooms, West Beach, Cromer (1950's).** A 1952 newspaper cutting - "Spend a restful and happy holiday at CROMER - a charming gem set midst the rugged beauty of the Norfolk coast. Abundant sunshine. Good walks .... Concert Party on the Pier .... in fact, everything for your enjoyment and comfort."

Cromer in the 1960's. 1966 official guide book - "Picture a long, broad, sandy beach - never dirty and never over-crowded .... this picture from the beach, of sparkling sea, sunlit sands, fishermen at work and children at play, is one that stays most vividly in the minds of the people who love Cromer."

Bibliography

C. Scott, "Poppyland Papers" (1886)

C. Scott, "Lays and Lyrics" (1888)

C. Scott, "Blossom Land and Fallen Leaves" (1890)

G. Parry, editor, "The Maid of the Mill" (1936)

G. Parry, "Leaves from an Overstrand Scrapbook,"
1962 (unpublished

A. Berlyn, "Vera in Poppyland" (1893-5)

A. C. Swinburne, "A Midsummer Holiday and Other
Poems" (1884)

L. Hoare, "Cromer Memories"

Lady Battersea, "Reminiscences" (1922)

E. Bartell, "A Guide to Cromer," 2nd Edition, (1806)

W. White, "History, Gazetteer, and Directory of
Norfolk . . . . " (1845), (1883)

"A Guide to Cromer," by a visitor (1867), (1878)

A. C. Savin, "History of Cromer" (1937)

A. Campbell Erroll, "A History of Sheringham and
Beeston Regis (1970)

P. Stibbons and D. Cleveland, "Poppyland, Strands
of Norfolk History" 1981

F. Stibbons, "In the King's Country" (1931)

M. Rouse, "Coastal Resorts of East Anglia" (1982)

E. Rose, "The Rise and Fall of Poppyland"
(N.A.R.G. News) (1978)

Illustrations

Peter Brooks Collection
15, 30, 53, 90, 111, 115, 121, 123, 129, 132, 133.

Cromer Museum
16, 21, 23, 25, 28, 29, 33, 36, 43, 67, 79, 93, 94, 95, 96, 97, 98, 100, 103, 104, 106, 110, 113, 128, 134, 138, 139, 145, 155, front cover.

Cyril Crawford Holden Collection
2, 3, 8, 9, 10, 11, 13, 14, 19, 24, 35, 37, 39, 40, 41, 42, 44, 49, 51, 52, 55, 58, 65, 69, 70, 74, 75, 76, 77, 81, 86, 88, 89, 91, 99, 105, 107, 109, 120, 154, 156, 159, 160, 161, 162, 163, Page 6

Jarrold and Sons
4, 5, 6, 7, 18, 20, 38, 45, 46, 47, 48, 57, 61, 62, 66, 68, 71, 72, 82, 83, 85, 87, 92, 101, 102, 108, 119, 131, 135, 141, 142, 143, 144, 146, 147, 148, 149, 150, 151, 152, 153

J. W. Mitchley
125, 127

Gwen Parry
26, 27

Poppyland Collection
1, 17, 22, 31, 32, 34, 50, 54, 56, 59, 60, 63, 64, 73, 78, 80, 84, 118, 122, 126, 130, 136, 137, 140, 157, 158, end paper photos

Poppyland Photos
112, 116, 117

Randall/Salter Magic Lantern Slide Collection
114

Real Photos
12

Jack Bryant, Poppyland Photos
Final Collage